3

They went down a long track and into a wood.

Erik had lots of snacks as they went.

The Long, Dark Trek

Written by
Cath Jones

Illustrated by
Dan Widdowson

Ransom

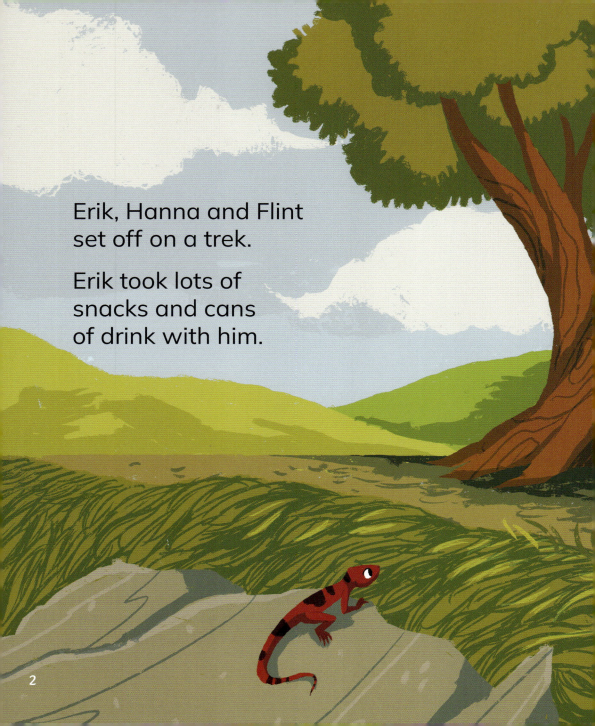

Erik, Hanna and Flint
set off on a trek.

Erik took lots of
snacks and cans
of drink with him.

He left litter on the track and
a drink can on a big tree stump.

A chill wind swept up the track. There was a thick frost on the trees.

"I think we're lost," Hanna said, "and soon it'll be dark!"

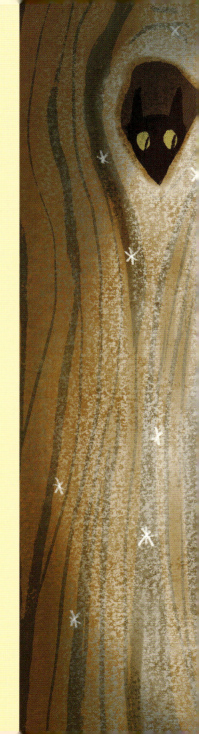

They crept down the track.

"We need to get out of this wood," said Flint. "But how?"

"Look!" Erik said. "What's that?"

It was a gang of litter pickers. They were picking up litter in the wood.

Erik, Hanna and Flint were so glad to see them.

"Greetings!" one of the litter pickers said to them.

"You can help us pick up all this litter. There's a lot of it on this track – it's such a mess."

Erik went a bit red.

"We are so glad to see you," said Flint. "We're lost. How do we get out of this wood?"

"Get out?" said the litter picker.
She was looking at the trail
of litter on the track.

15

"That's no problem at all.

Look, there's a town, right next to the track!"